THAT OUR EYES BE RIGGED

Kristi Maxwell

saturnalia books

Distributed by University Press of New England
Hanover and London

Saturnalia Books
105 Woodside Rd.
Ardmore, PA 19003
info@saturnaliabooks.com

ISBN: 978-0-9915454-1-4
Library of Congress Control Number: 2014945132

Book Design by Saturnalia Books
Printing by McNaughton & Gunn

Cover Art: *River Water* by Noah Saterstrom, mixed media on paper, 2013.

Author Photo: Jason McLean

Distributed by:
University Press of New England
1 Court Street
Lebanon, NH 03766
800-421-1561

My thanks to the editors of the following journals in which many of these poems first appeared: *Action, Yes!, Coconut, Court Green, The Equalizer, Forklift, Ohio, Handsome, Konundrum Engine Literary Review, Microfilme, The Modern Review, Octopus, Peacock Online Review, RealPoetik, Saltgrass, Swine, Transom,* and *Word for/Word.*

"One Name Would Be Enough To Exorcise This Astonishment" was recorded for episode six of *Rabbit Light Movies*. An excerpt from "Tiny Wires Touching the Right Way" appeared as a broadside through *Practice: New Writing & Art* under a different title.

My gratitude to those who spent time with these poems in their various stages and coaxed me and them along: Michael Rerick, Jillian Weise, Ashley VanDoorn, Christian Hawkey, and the poets of various Wedges + Lines: Brett Price, Megan Martin, Lesley Jenike, Evan Commander, Bo McGuire, Matt Hart, Cindy King, Ruth Williams, Joe DeLong, Ellen Elder, Eric Bliman, Jesseca Cornelson, Heather Hamilton, Matt McBride, Dana Ward, Joshua Butts, and Lisa Ampleman. Thanks to Henry Israeli and the Saturnalia Books staff. Deepest love to James Pihakis, Sara Leah Miller, Leslie Wylie, Leah Willis, Betsy Pinkerton West, and Kristen Nelson, whose friendships have helped me write and think. I remain indebted to the support of my family, Marilyn, Ken, Jennifer, and Lori.

TABLE OF CONTENTS

IN WHICH WE ASK, EXIST

Light chews on the patio
or could
a jawbone of light invents a countenance
to settle its valley, to climb scalp-ward
a jawbone of light exposes the whole
pitiable face
juts out over some poor domain
some poor dark domain
I've taken a bar into my thought
borrowed thoughts
barred my better thoughts
thought better of
doing that one thing

The patio wears braces of light
to right itself
a string singing light
throttling the throat of darkness
straddling and riding the darkened throat
spur to flesh, reins ripping up
the soft floor of some hands

I want to speak into the library door
and enter—to speak the library into existence
to pick the speck of book off a tongue
to tongue an exit
to enter and leave simultaneously
I want I want I want

If a couch scalps the room
we are follicles growing from it
loosening and scattering
being picked up by someone
and tossed aside
the way of boats
in the narrative
of the worst storm

Hold the struggling bird in your ear
Hold its struggle away from its body
Take the bread tie from the sack of bread
the hunger from the feeding
the hunger from the feeling

Let us sit inside the weather
Let us be a slice each
going bad
inside this bag of weather
the rain has forgotten about
failing to eat us
We will grow new things
gross things
and they will be beautiful
you will be beautiful in the gross light
growing from me
from the grocery of light
make your purchase
in the aisle of light
pursue me

Or simply to make one purr with a light touch
to use our hands
to wear our hands in an outdated style
of kindness
bang always above the eye
A head bruised by wood
A heart bruised by what would

Eye the bird struggling against the grate
soot-body ash-body panic-animated
Exhaust yourself
please exhaust yourself
little punctuation mark of
bird that is ending me

After weaning the blankets of their warm.

Weeks warp in like cheap siding, aluminum

or what would be wood to the eye

that doesn't know wood well.

The little cat sleeping looks so.

An armchair full of hairs and the little cat's sleeping

like a longest hair. We await the ritual

of the shed.

ONE NAME WOULD BE ENOUGH TO EXORCISE THIS ASTONISHMENT

The year melting performed ache's snow version followed, serendipitously, our toast: That sadness will not star in every wet episode of the head! Sold on rapture, we named two pups "blessing" and "blessing" and called them both to us and hid our surprise at their coming.

Once more the press is eluded through stowing. Stowed in the carcass of a colt. Draw the curtains, they ask, and we assess our needles and nod.

For the tract built into the abstract, what might be excrement to fill it the way a white screen set in the amphitheater's jaw? A white screen filled with dresses the plot tends.

We said want which minted need. Said sated and wedded it. Still, we say desire is a mean need and mean—what? That. Our jar reeks of the manicured field.

It took mining the hog's fatty jewels—gristly shinys—to learn skin's function as frame. Later, the unction of frames: if empty, deliberately, empty decks the eye with awe. Should the eye still stand. Oh that our eyes be rigged that emptiness would not best us based on display.

We stick to things we are quick to. The field's dialogue goes like this: trough, trough. And, yes, the answers in the shape of cows, in the shape of hogs to which we cluck sweetly.

How well we know the pail came down to inventing water. And, yet, our hands.

For the sensibility the sprinkler brings, should we reconsider? Were not an apostrophe the sole bridle we'd found. Let's add this to the gold-leafed pronunciation key of our defeats. Beside "Wheat fields say nothing. Which is sad."

It was not just minutiae that paused us.

TO KEEPING WE DID NOT FORGET

This was the point
of excursion—where throats opened like the upside of canoes.
Little launches dazzled the banks after the mining
of our crisp bags.

To navigate recreation and hunger.
To navigate we string water with steer.

Not the colts' nostrils for our tracing, but

air hung
with manifestations
we tracked
to a lively source.

Plus this small insistence

a fern ignored on the patio to basket and a clod
of dead things.

Our hands were out for this and for the
execution of each rotted board
the decades made

Bright lab of our insolence

*

To script itineraries by how
houses connect
by décor. The well-shaped bone

we felt up the field to find.
Some tack, some wire, an abrupt morning,
and the thrum collected in our knee
shed its singing
deep in the basin

of Epsom maxed out with warmth.
Our bodies maxed out

then the cutting up: our last age.

In the story we recited with frequency and evening
a forest guffaws and three foxes appear.
A forest guffaws and four foxes appear.

Evidence

repetition corners relation

and all the missing calves.

Rain mythologized the runt kittens we left for it—myth-instruments

for soldering
such solitary attention to a given day or days
given a week to play out
given a week to pay out to history.

So as not to dizzy ourselves, bulls-eyes decorate each room.
We focus. We converse like trapped birds
and windowpanes or deep cherry panels along
the ceiling.

*

When does consequence cease to mean?
The lake too full and the fish

coddled through our
swimming and the fish we could catch in our hands.

A small fire stuns the field within cinder blocks.
The field looks far away

in this narrow perception of light.

Narrow procession, we pad our way behind
at a distance so as not to be with, nor construed as with
though we know no one watches

so pad closer.
We even close in like a type of commerce one moment
before backing away. An earnest probability

is all we asked of any garden.

*

Optimally, rocks we managed to off
onto the flatbed first indebted the field

through aeration.

Vests were learned third
as a thing

to remove.

Vests were removed from our view

We, articulate as husk-snap, compared it to harvest.
And thus how we knew nude was this

Modesty gleaned from fields.

So novel our acuity, it outdid our dearest machines.

& WE TAKE AS FROM MARROW

Come now.

We had just finished saying.

Had finished it.

In the bed decked out with sleeping, its attendant vision
fans and fans. We take fat bottles

we take fat jars unto morning and under the belly
to white-out these things with response
and tugging. Each body builds hymns
like machinery, so with purpose. To turn ourselves on

and blast
over the speakers mounted atop
the poles. Good nests.

Our gorging endeavors to separate us

from our hunger

—but to case out and sass excess!

What did we mean by that like a final pledge?

And our teeth we hung like a caption above the tendered meat.
We who hang out at the bone

courtesy of and within curtsies we train into our flanks

alongside corporeal. How the bales meant both and either
in the spare molecule of the loft.

Though the auctioneer seldom baffles
our ear as he used to.
And that

each new crop commands the barracks set at the edge
of needing

we have begun using our fists again

Distorted plows.

We rig the pipes with denim
cinched there
and water

falls into the arena
like a last rose which is compromise
and picked up.

This is our flailing opposition—

this our free pound of grout.

We wear our arms out
like lent jewelry—we
and their glistening

The cause of glisten nearby.

*

With the import of an amulet,
the shattered

thing lets us in
on its presence.

Gravel we sift through to collect.

Small fins of a boon

eagerly, miserly
we note and grip

that this is final
-ly

a display we will push past
for all angles.

To embrace this
means also to have lodge

and the obstruction potential in that.

PLAISIR MINUS

+/-

How absolutely right of you, how appallingly right on at that time to say it—Fraud. I have finally worn out the shirt I wore out when you said it before—we were out of the car. A fraud again—I sold the shirt. Pit-withered or whether it is worn out, complacently, to a place, I cannot place it this way, my guessing sullied through the sale. That honor of the owner, to place the wearing in a where. The man you humored at the bar was my wife, married to my husband thought. You thought I had no husband. Chose not to implicate my husband in your calling—fraud.

Rather easily one can recall certain seats she sat in beside certain others (and certain others, a curtain de-certains a discerning). Who is what depends on direction—the director determining form and where from. From the stage (the actor cannot sieve a say, yet appeases the peevish spotlight with such gutted articulation), the first syllable in this instance of remembering is our sitting beside one another like stresses, or unstressed, but set off by the stress.

I won't to say I love you. I certainly won't—
to say I love you—do anything with my
mouth. I want to wind my mouth up to say. I
didn't. My mouth wasn't wound. Wasn't
wound. Bloodied with saying. Fraud! My
mouth defended. Fender mouth that rammed
yonder saying. Near the cow guards. The
sheep grates. Near the bones that nary should
have passed. Pasted up, the Great Mouth that
passes through once a year—for which we will
pay.

Which point has reached its boiling. At which point? Gyozas we stuffed with kimchi. I'd have it easier, recollection, recalling the you I knew if you were dead and thus outside my knowing. The now in my knowing. Dead recollection. Rather than this. Doing as we did. Did with the potential of do—because you're off somewhere, you-ing. How we pressed each satchel. Secure. Each edge depressed by our fingers. Impressed (with). After those entered our mouths. A recipe I look for—to make without. Without thinking about, but the taste.

If one maps her road trip. If one maps her road trip so cities are signified by chicken wings. If one wings it from city to city based on a survey of chicken wings. Based on which is best and which location this which is is in. That's it. Followed by another it. An it-ditty. Oh isn't it pretty, oh isn't it.

A highway lined with mattresses. Fraud!—
you've caught me again. A median meditative
as one mattress as thought-bubble shows. One
point cannot make a line unless that point is
line-shaped. Fat line a mattress makes. Or if
that point is lined as with a sheet, though in
this case, not. Naked mattress no one points
out as. I think now we should have pointed to
the mattress and pointedly said, Mattress, go
get a room. Some sham! To have shamed it for
falling. For slipping from the ropes we tied so
tightly that others who looked at our tying
said, Yes, that should do.

What a bunch of crap—brunch exchanged for a small thing. Yogurt-sized or actual. My frauding caught like something stationary. To talk through it. Concussion-through. Not a discarded roll toilet paper scrolled from to empty. Though this was empty. Little concussions of the heart that resulted in— not loss, not the golden floss memory shows off as. The sweater I've sewn from that day. Bah, bah little sheep, little wealth sheep that keeps our record in its teeth—our cud.

COMBS

Amidst what classifies the bag as crammed, hair implements take a little space that constitutes a world for them to know through their showing up there.

I bask.

My hair tarries high as a barometer that measures my basking.

I bask in this life this only life I have unless only is not the life-slot that takes my token in. That takes my kin yet leaves me?

Someone pointed out I stole his brush several years after I stole it.

This knack for taking things like brushes out of homes is mine.

Because there is a certain, determined amount of pride imbedded in mine, I bask in that knack for mining things.

Intermingling is not something the language realm and the physical realm always do.

Like wallflowers at the same party, off somewhere fondling a hair implement such as an elastic band, they are not always mingling.

A public restroom with what looks like a dresser that belongs in a private space has on that dresser a vase of combs that are implied to be complimentary, given their plastic nature and the name of the bar of which the public restroom is part imprinted in white on each of the green combs.

I bask when I snatch one as I wade into a stall.

Some plastic can heal itself.

Some plasma-savvy can't.

Preference happens. Like and unlike growth of hair.

If choice quits preference, we might call that particular choice hairless.

We might not.

One of us might.

It is a choice we will make, each having inherently to do with language.

It is a choice we will each make—having, inherently.

I bask as if basking were invented for me.

I verb, and that verb fills itself with the action known as basking.

MY COST,

as I've decided to

address you, before the bovine

lullaby begins. I drank milk during the writing of,

as I wrote it, so there's that

kind of gleam. Two new

muscles show in my arm. A case my upper

arm displays of muscles new

to me, but old to lifting. Line

with a sole cursive letter with

multiple humps. What can we catch like this

nothing? With hooks diluted

of shine by small rusts?

I tire as tall things

their indulgence of hangings. This

chair fashioned, this stoop. This sweeping of

the stoop for the dropping. The only

note the fan's achieved is

whirr, but don't chide, but

facilitate the fan with wind chimes it can

whirr through: we're, we're. The two

of them a wee, a whoa, a giddy-up.

The gangly noon fondles the spade, and I've still

not found the shawl. To draw out the crash I need

five colors in marker-form and the sleek

dormitories of my fingers for shaping

to lean from. The fist-char

charges through this accumulation we've laid over

the towel rack over the panoramic

tiles. It is not a question. There's the passing

out like larger tiles in a larger room.

And the crosshatch reasons for attachment, and one of us

must water before we test, one of us must

hands under it. Spackling made

ache of the egg without outing the egg as art, true or—

I always want to say falsetto to sing it true in falsetto.

A shin kick won't wrench my standing

for this: truth reared in some

intolerant bowel. Were I made to

eat a hoof. Were we made with heft that could

take on the meanest jaw, then might

we asunder. On the bed all day today, and the bed

boogies away from Earth to get a different

calendar. One bed day is. Two bed days

is my dorsal fin that divides

water to incidence. We were in.

So taken. Going forgone for this.

When I

said deliver

me I

meant deliver as

over the

falls a man

stuffed crate

MINED

IT WAS THAT OLD MASS YEARNING FOR A LIKENESS IN ALL THINGS THAT TROUBLED

I miss my guess—the lungs were placed in water, sinking, and while the one he drove was winter, the wonder and the thrill. Out of the tail of his eye, whenever he is. Her jaw became a trifle set; in this special way it is of the earth's earthy. She bruised under her heel the scaly head of this dark suspicion. There were phases of this thing: "his gray" felt "shoes." Took his eye: a felon little more than a compound with a long prayer and by the wife.

A VERY MINOR DEPARTMENT OF THIS

For they would nudge one another, true to the standard or to type, he felt himself of labor, a silly who. Instead of brighter because of this. It was plainly necessary—the thing marvelous- marvelous. A joy-night supper. They is some young overhead on this night, refined—the compliment stuck still moods. Blacked up, very little, I was all in. But the jaw itself, care-stamped with the privilege of two others. Dark vignette of wood she was not. He liked and he did not like this exact request of the very large concern he was seeking full cousin to. Rattle and clatter of ratchet arms armed with taking. With this mistering, some character-building plan. She merely beamed a fatty beam with the soft needles so long climbing up to it.

THAT WHICH IS THE INHERITANCE

A third hymn was indulged in—a somewhat more lengthy but no less nondescript highway. He never had had. One who fingers savagely at a material knot and yet cannot undo it. In disassociating God from harm and error and misery, the wiseacre who makes money make things go. This would sear. The very teeth of a grave. None of the compulsion of the practical, just a fairly representative scene. But this other black barrier he himself had built! To himself adding: "Had he?" A task in part the tissue of lies. To seal, as closing waters—rough-hew them how we may! To make a clean breast of all that.

OF THEM

It was none of these places

we joked about a tower of towels.

Whether one is *in* or *at* a park, and if the same distinguishes whether two.

Baby wipes buried in a bag for mud-letting.

His pristine hands, a flesh chapel hid behind the scaffolding of open-fingered gloves.

~

At home, a flat tire keeps him there.

Rosy-red fingers smashed in chrome.

Not At Home collects three parks in one name.

Singly called The First Below Zero Night, Sludge, and Where Ice Splices Throats to Laughter.

~

There are many steps for stepping through a park.

Ours include: performing leisurely with little applause.

The way snow comes down.

A chin dipping to a chest to close the busy drawbridge under which gusts rush.

Rails attempt to ease the tension between ice and humans.

My hand lodges like a splinter in the grove.

The rail is for people who are not parks.

Binoculars for flight, for *with* to enter in the outside we're outside of.

~

Billed at the top of a hill are mirrors built as a maze that bullies reflections.

In this one, he is an entire spade of grass a camera lens plays bee toward and zooms.

A mirror is a park where light picnics.

Where light dines on refraction.

In my favorite, I construe his teeth a caravan because they are still the way a gaze is, projecting out.

~

To write about parks the way he walks through them.

To stalk his walking through the scrawny page park I pen.

About parks, about parks, about parks, I write, park, parked, will park, I write, furiously, and with homage.

~

Milling around with mulled wine warming our hands, we pass on benches.

We pass our gloved hands from one pocket then the next to the other's and the other's other.

~

Snow erases mud our feet rewrite.

Snow and mud and our feet plunged and our feet plugged into our shoes and snow and mud a feat to plough through and we do.

Slipping, we separate and our separating is a colon between us.

We who number who digital clock and set ourselves for this occasion.

POST

We outline our bellies with the belly in the plural
not ours. The role of
club to the other's seal,

and wear it. A resurrection machine that isn't womb-built
nor stilted toward cells.
The museum's stopped closing

all together. Someone has covered his hands in light and repeats
my light hands, my light hands
assumed light even

before. Burlap otherwise claimed
as the sleep-post denotes
is stashed in some other arctic
not amassed to land.

Outdone by oil jiggling with glisten, the mouth
whose enlightenment jig is up
shows off its small screens. Over which what moves.

What isn't ensued by viewing and proven
after. Water muscled by waves
caught in the tide muzzle. This intended restraint

our tending is the refrain for. Swoosh
that drug-busts muteness again.

TO EXERCISE THIS ASTONISHMENT

My voice is gussied up with the gaudiness of requesting.

Our ships as a pox on the sea.

I have misread holies as fired toward and dressed obliteration as get down.

Bravo leaflets fine-tuned with fear stashed in the font's darkest rooms.

Bravo until the transparency of use.

Set the jingle on praise and call forth our sweeter appraiser to announce us prepared and worthy conduits.

Magnificent shell set against the face; magnificence that muzzles us.

Reluctant to give up the three dead crabs, I find a fourth and sew a dirge.

Hands bob in several rooms.

Prayer as the one who and her doing.

I pray nibbling betray no new mice for my trapping and that my love not squirm in the trappings of my slight fingers, that I not slight my love with refusal.

To ask brings the impact of drought if this land shows our need.

To dilute the parade of spectators without complaint or the pause of our supple horns.

Pander is the bear in the zoo of our most likely deceptions; the bear we wave to and feed.

Repentance duty does not obfuscate, doing that refuses duty, do fused to will flounders with the knife by which one is offered up through the off-ing.

Sorrow we waive

suffers through hallelujah.

On the backs of heat-slicked horses we shine like no thing or like it is no thing to do so.

An antique lapel holds court for blue ribbons as evidence of application, of applying oneself toward and the inevitable win.

And so a breeze is how we understand a compliment to the coming cool.

Itinerant broom stagnated by such flawless tile, socks again, our socks against the august notion.

The violence of a bell.

The glint of a belle.

We share with her each guise of tea.

And the collective mouth for serving.

Bright, we answer first and loudly when asked to describe; we have learned what illumination omits from character, we have learned what fools her needles best, and we use our learning as sea foam to hook some typed-up shore.

She scatters fame over the graves.

A model car bolted to stone and a doll we carve a hand to dole out to eternal.

Sweet abacus hung like antlers amused with flies we count; we count, ridiculous we, we've found a job to account for our existing.

Mais oui a new job.

Interpreter bankrupt of omens.

I have photographed my birthmark from five angles to submit, and I watch to see my submission scrutinized with care.

She bathes in our interest that unplugs fountains.

It is like this daily, and when it is not, desire's finally conjured, and the world's ankle folds and snaps to secure its bed rest.

Wind packs our flapping shirts.

We dedicate ourselves to each alarm, battle the braying with response.

In each discarded shoebox, she anchors a sunset, and our awe is our confession.

That we could calculate moods to solve any scenario.

To shift the fountain to the thirst.

For whose notorious blindness we enact a different sense, thine eyes clouded over and no udder from which freed might be the what watt-ed with contemplation.

She flickers last in the bulb.

THAT WHOSE HUGENESS

translates to buoyancy

translates to huge in relation to how it will bog

the tidy mouth

Bird as boat sinks in the wire shoreline assured

by need

for electricity near houses

Imitable hugeness borne of intimidation of space

A planet holds its own

through light

Bone of light our telescopes dress

with viewing

Garnished eye

Once we were in a house

with situational teas

that teased our choice this way

to have near lake surface decoupaged with sleeves

and something about a stockyard (or was it staunch yard)

where action stalked "to have"

and "had" refused such nuzzling

despite our sipping

crippled by the cup's depth

Lacking hands

the fuse counters or accounts for

something

scripted for the switch

Off and On are learned if not expected

to mean Off and On

though often they mean the gesture

that leads to one of two things

TINY WIRES TOUCHING THE RIGHT WAY

"Where is the body that is prepared to receive language?"
Nathalie Stephens, *Touch To Affliction*

A pharynx / A fox clot / A fever
How do you say again
How do you dew a morning
and / or
do a mourning

with / (out) / adieu

How to
A fair nixed / A caput / A clap put on for validation / Valet of praise
and we'll park you / we'll ark you / and awe
The macaw shuns the corn / honeys the having of else

That the oar in fact divides the water conjunction-like
That the oar in fact divvies the water between steer and still

*

Swish was a sound you made / how
You made how from your / No, no oven / No buzz
nor out nor / narwhal

a certain padding sea offers beach / a pudding / of foam
Where does light sleep when a peach is laid open
and its juice that attracts refraction / a fiction

of glowing having

Of glow halving a second time
and the eye gagging for it / for the gorge / The eye gagged
with gorgeous / with just the image of

With the image of just

*

A see / A seem / A sleigh and / and / or slight
A slender / A cylinder / A seal endures, but the whale-jowl /
the water jabbed with chase / The hasten / The Hades

your first gone teeth were thrown into / for luck
against losing / for loose sing that flabs up an ear as would it / a room

*

Cyborg : / Board of sighs where we pin our own breaths like tails /
so a party / this sewn party you wear / for those to knock at /
for those noggins to enter and with / gin to enter
the noggin hole / a whole rabbit with / little ice paws to scratch
the glass / let me in / let me in

*

Phyllo for a low fee and frozen / for a low fee for a bread-based leaf

To take the lead which is the tongue for sure / Ma soeur / Mon
frère / Taste reared in the pan / sold to the pink pink
to the glistening / Groom of meat

on which meat is laid / Don't say it / Incest / Don't
say it I insist / I sister / Cyst that grew in the you-tourist /
the uterus / of the family tree

*

And this one a sleeping pearl / And this one
a sloughed purl / both purring

End is an exquisite form of melt
End is an exit / Being being a requisite for

Josh was a kid / is a kidding / To kid
and not / reproduce / Produce in the placenta-cart

A cent / A scent / A century churned in the belly
of believe me / of history / A lie, no a li(f)e / no lives or known lives
excluded / Invite only / Bon anni

No is / they insist / But how a be without it / How an insist /
How a be-day party / For which as promised / cupcakes stabbed
with verbs / and huffing and puffing and down, down

cramming each pillow / for each heady no to rest

*

Wrote a prettiest dress / a dress arrested whose
nakedness / If clothes erase
bodies / who draws them back / Shed left
a stencil on the floor / Who traced it

*

Crocus / Pro-fuss / Grow a cuss out
of this toe-stub / this fender / some harmless
boo / lube some eyes with temper / Timber goes

your cool / Gossamer / Gossiper / Sip up
and spew the latest / to ladle out / to un-dull

listen / that your guests might undulate / in squeal /
that your in-the-know acts the squirrel / on the
electric wire / boredom / dons / to amuse itself / "I'm not

bored" / it says / "but electric wire / made to shiver /
make me shiver" / Well / make it / well /

in your telling / your tailing of current / of / is it? /
of yes / surely / surly yes, so surly

Be thou / all / and me / accused and accuser / curse
amusement / an amusement curse / cast / for us / our own

Bippity Boppity / Wand / and Wound / Out Which
Pus Flies / in its Sparkle-Guise / Eww Converted to Ooh

*

Squirts of time / full-fisted squirts of it

Mustard / Must herd the time
to retard it with rope / to tether it to the heaviest
cart / that Do can construct for plowing
the minute field / the very small / with infinitesimal
husks / budding with asks / bake such requests
with your politest sun / your cheek

The dear an I is / eyelets still as deer / or shaped
like parts of them

*

To locate in joy / in general / oneself
For the guess to manhandle the hope / with accuracy / with
occurrence / Guess eased into yes / into visitor /

visor / -ed advisor / bouncer to light
lined up / within lines / that shape a bulb
near the bulb / where the neck necks
with collarbone / Turn-on

Turn awning into what eyes do / in shame / If these
eyes are caskets / If kits / and to repair
through re- / pairing

*

Software / Gently worn / Soft wear
given it / The perfect jeans fjord your body / figure it

wear history / we're through
I certainly need

To stutter home / to stud home with "remain"

cartilage of a valley / where ourselves
are the sticking thing / or / it's sticky

the reason for each leave
to reason leavening a progress / a program
of rise

darkening that chews up a stage with hands / handling
bravo / addled by the bling

our attention is / piled on the neck
of a hunch / we accomplice / our guess spliced
to a reasoning / resin of perhaps

My soul's in your head

if anywhere. The song

said so or something

like it. I fold my voice

to fit your ear. I fold it

more compactly

and store it. Stalled

after all. What horse

is this—that carries us

one at a time?

EVERY TIME I WANT TO WRITE YOU,
I'M GOING TO WRITE A LINE INSTEAD:

Something in contrast to brightness, this dark mood
the picture of a glacier now circulating
eclipsed by a ship—perhaps, serendipitously, a snow
He has been gathering
the smallest toiletries
to take away
This habit of cleaning
clearing the face
Face cleared of expression
Man cleared of the charge
Woman cleared   clear
The charge between us depleted by words
A face pleated by an excess of laughter
A right amount
Perhaps, serendipitously
flash makes snow of your face
I will ball myself
clean   drag a cotton ball
drag a cotton raft to a carpet of tears
tear a carpet up for what's hard underneath
For what's hard underneath?
For what on the surface is hard
We move between plentitude and impoverishment
Some expedition
among the ones that fail

EVERY TIME I WANT TO WRITE YOU, I'M GOING TO WRITE A LINE INSTEAD:

Thank you for being generative
generous   I have all these lines
like a happy cokehead
Gathered my eyes
about a photograph of an infant and a dog
both on their respective mats
backs to each other
A set of malformed lungs
There is a biscuit contest somewhere
A contested biscuit
This business of shutting down
Name three empty things
A person can't really be empty
so a person doesn't count
Of course I do not believe that
people don't count

EVERY TIME I WANT TO WRITE YOU, I'M GOING TO WRITE A LINE INSTEAD:

Interested in creases

Increases, decreases

the space where a leg folds

knee-wise and where

a leg meets the crotch

My interest increases

Interested in crotchety as an adjective

In who fits what word

In who fights what word

In fighting words

Them fighting words

Us fighting words

Us fighting

A first fight and a last fight

A fist fight or a word fight

What's worth a fight

The struggle to feel one's worth

EVERY TIME I WANT TO WRITE YOU, I'M GOING TO WRITE A LINE INSTEAD:

I have a leak
which is preferable to crying
Have a leak and know the language of repair
Know numbers to call
No numbers to call
Bingo! Yesterday a set of earrings
made of records were wrapped
Set on the path
to make rapt
a set of ears
I hate
what one word
from the right mouth
can do
To wish a mouth
leak   to be licked by a word
Word! Exclamation, reclamation—
air stitched reparations to an ear
I as the distance between waiting and wafting
I as what pierces wanting
through with waiting

EVERY TIME I WANT TO WRITE YOU, I'M GOING TO WRITE A LINE INSTEAD:

The privilege of choosing
not to eat or to eat
Of having to remind oneself
to eat
Of being reminded by the body's sounds
and so eating because able
and so eating at a table
A rhyme reveals an uncanny relation
Jotted in a margin: pois'd/moist
Liked the look of the apostrophe
A false eyelash affixed to a letter
That's as far as that can go
Shortened rather than lengthened
Strange desire
for an eye "to pop"
Kernel of an eye   for grazing
for getting lodged
The carnal eye
We take it as far as it can go

NOTES

"In Which We Ask, Exist" is for Jason McLean.

The title "One Name Would Be Enough To Exorcise/This
Astonishment" is a variation on a line in Roland Barthes' The Pleasure of
the Text: "One name would be enough to exorcise his astonishment."
The quote toward the end of the poem is taken from Antoine de Saint-
Exupéry's *The Little Prince* (Richard Howard's translation).

The lines that make up the series "Mined" are distortions, modifications,
or borrowings of phrases and clauses from Theodore Dreiser's *An
American Tragedy*.

Winners of the Saturnalia Books Poetry Prize:

Thieves in the Afterlife by Kendra DeColo
Lullaby (with Exit Sign) by Hadara Bar-Nadav
My Scarlet Ways by Tanya Larkin
The Little Office of the Immaculate Conception by Martha Silano
Personification by Margaret Ronda
To the Bone by Sebastian Agudelo
Famous Last Words by Catherine Pierce
Dummy Fire by Sarah Vap
Correspondence by Kathleen Graber
The Babies by Sabrina Orah Mark

Also Available from saturnalia books:

Don't Go Back to Sleep by Timothy Liu
Reckless Lovelys by Martha Silano
A spell of songs by Peter Jay Shippy
Each Chartered Street by Sebastian Agudelo
No Object by Natalie Shapero
Nowhere Fast by William Kulik
Arco Iris by Sarah Vap
The Girls of Peculiar by Catherine Pierce
Xing by Debora Kuan
Other Romes by Derek Mong
Faulkner's Rosary by Sarah Vap
Gurlesque: the new grrly, grotesque, burlesque poetics edited by Lara Glenum and Arielle Greenberg
Tsim Tsum by Sabrina Orah Mark
Hush Sessions by Kristi Maxwell
Days of Unwilling by Cal Bedient

Letters to Poets: Conversations about Poetics, Politics, and Community
edited by Jennifer Firestone and Dana Teen Lomax

Artist/Poet Collaboration Series:

Velleity's Shade by Star Black / Artwork by Bill Knott
Polytheogamy by Timothy Liu / Artwork by Greg Drasler
Midnights by Jane Miller / Artwork by Beverly Pepper
Stigmata Errata Etcetera by Bill Knott / Artwork by Star Black
Ing Grish by John Yau / Artwork by Thomas Nozkowski
Blackboards by Tomaz Salamun / Artwork by Metka Krasovec

That Our Eyes Be Rigged was printed using the fonts Kabel and Adobe Garamond Pro.

www.saturnaliabooks.org